Self-Ta

The Proven Concept Of Breaking Free From Intense Negative Thoughts To Never Feel Weak Again

By

Stuart Wallace

Table of Contents

Introduction

Are you hounded by relentless thoughts about how you are a failure, or how you screwed up yet again, or how you are not good enough? Are you tired of being depressed, anxious, and full of self-blame? Do you lie awake at night, thinking horrible things about yourself? Have your relationships or even your health suffered as a result of your persistent unhappy thinking?

I understand your fear that you will never be happy again. For months or even years, perhaps for your whole life, you have been unhappy. Your head is full of ugly thoughts that promptly obliterate any joy you do experience. What you are suffering from is negative self-talk.

You can and will feel happiness again. The reason why is that your mind is malleable and you can restructure your self-talk to bring about more positivity. This process does not happen overnight. It requires some effort on your part and a series of psychologist-formulated techniques that you will learn in the following pages.

This book is not just another "Be Happy" listicle. I read plenty of those listicles when I was struggling with low self-esteem and depression, and while the advice contained in them was usually sensible, they never did much good. This is because they didn't teach the fundamentals of self-talk psychology and how to get to the root of the habits that drive negative self-talk.

When I was finally fed up with being unhappy, I sought the help of cognitive behavioral therapy. I learned that I could perform many techniques on my own without an expensive therapist, so I set about finding the best techniques that actually offered me relief. After consulting a myriad of psychology journals and CBT guides, I finally found a solution to my poor thinking habits. Now I am here to present my findings to you.

Your self-talk drives how you think, feel, and act. It is the linguistic instructions that your mind gives to you as you go about your day. When you change your self-talk to something positive, you will see every area of your life change for the better. You will start to see the good in yourself, and you will start to love yourself. You will be able to forgive and fix your mistakes. People will start to enjoy being around you more, so your relationships will improve and you will make more friends. As you enrich your career with enthusiasm and eagerness to go to the next level, you will reap much more financial success. You will even tackle projects you have put off and make your dreams come true.

Psychologists have long understood that positive self-talk is helpful for people to engage in. That's why many psychologists have dedicated their careers to creating techniques to alter cognitive patterns and bring about more positive thinking. The results are proof that this approach works. Depression patients have managed to cure their conditions with positive self-talk. Olympic athletes and NBA players use self-talk to make big wins. People have even beat cancer just by changing the content of their self-monologues!

I promise that by the end of this book, you will know all of the techniques that will permanently change your self-talk for the better. If you put these techniques into action, then you will notice the rewards immediately. Your life will change into something greater than you ever imagined.

Don't wait. You have been unhappy for too long already. Since life is short, you should use the time you have now to make your dreams come true and enjoy being you. Read on to learn how to unlock your true potential with positive self-talk.

Chapter 1: Positive Self-Talk, The Negative Thought Eliminator

Positive self-talk is the core of happiness and high self-esteem. But negative self-talk is just the opposite. The purpose of positive self-talk is to regulate your inner dialogue to eliminate negative, self-defeating beliefs and unlock your true potential as a human being.

Negative self-talk is something that most people are naturally prone to due to a combination of environmental and genetic factors. It is basically a habit that can have extremely toxic effects on your overall attitude and life. Changing your self-talk is imperative for you to gain happiness and well-being.

First, learn about the problem and what it does to you, in order to gain motivation to eliminate negative thinking from your brain. The key to fixing any problem is understanding it thoroughly. Only then can you see the need to change and go about making those changes.

What Is Negative Self-Talk?

You know that narrative that runs in your head? "You can't do this, so why are you even trying?" "They must think I'm such an idiot." "She would never go out with me." "I need to get out of here because I'm way out of my element." Scolding yourself, making self-defeating statements to yourself, or telling yourself that life sucks are all examples of bad narrative.

That is negative self-talk in a nutshell.

Your self-talk is simply the way you talk to yourself inside of your head. The voice in your head that whispers wisdom can also whisper some pretty self-limiting and discouraging things. The voice may imitate your abusive parent, or your deepest insecurities, or your most denigrating boss, coach, or teacher.

The thing most people don't realize is that the self-talk you play in your own mind is taught, starting with your role models and parental figures in childhood [1]. It can also be altered in time by the people you surround yourself with and the experiences you go through in life. It is a fluid thing that changes with exposure to different environmental factors.

Therefore, self-talk can certainly be restructured to be more positive. Through repeated models in your environment, you learned how to think about yourself and life in a negative way. Now you can reframe that thinking in a more positive form with new models.

You might wonder why you should bother doing this. Well, the real question is, Why shouldn't you? Negative self-talk has been found to be the number one aggravator of issues like depression, anxiety, low self-esteem, and fear [2]. It has been found to create significant mental stress, which in turn is harmful to your physical health and impairing for your life performance [2]. Often, negative self-talk is comprised of several cognitive distortions, or improper ways of thinking that make life seem darker than it really is [2]. In other words, the way you are thinking is making you feel awful and it also may be causing or exacerbating any mental illnesses you may have.

This does not mean that you are to blame for your own suffering. You learned negative self-talk, and at the present moment, it is all you know. However, there is a fantastic solution that you can do yourself or with the help of a coach or therapist, so why not do it? By changing negative self-talk, you can start to correct the thinking patterns, or cognitive distortions, that underlie your problems.

Self-talk is how your mind harnesses language to regulate your behavior [3]. Think of how you might tell yourself, "Take a left up here" as you drive. Your arm follows that direction and turns the steering wheel left. When you are under social stress, such as at a job interview, that self-talk tells you what to do and say to win the job. Really, self-talk is quite necessary for your daily functioning.

Thus, it follows that negative self-talk instructs you to act negatively, which can have some detrimental effects on your overall life. Meanwhile, more positive self-talk has the opposite, and more desirable, effect.

We all have an inner critic that upholds us to higher standards. This critic is not always bad, provided that you look for solutions to your subpar work as opposed to beating yourself up mentally [3]. It is also not realistic to expect to be chipper and happy all of the time. Sometimes, dark moods and ugly thoughts will cloud your mind, obliterating the sunshine and rainbows. However, you don't need to live in a storm all of the time. Learning to change your negative self-talk can make you feel happier and more proactive, which in turn can exponentially improve your quality of life.

What Are The Causes Of Negative Self-Talk?

Negative self-talk has been recognized as a major factor in poor sports performance and low self-esteem since the 1990s, with some studies highlighting its significance even earlier. A focus of cognitive behavioral therapy, most psychologists and therapists understand that self-talk is critical your overall mental health and outlook on life.

However, the exact causes of negative self-talk are not as clear. There are many studies that have attempted to unlock the true causes. They have shed some light on possible reasons that people may engage in negative self-talk.

The first and foremost currently understood idea is that self-talk is taught through environment. The influences that shape your mind when you are young, ranging from parents to school staff, can certainly affect the way you talk to yourself as you get older [4]. For instance, in a study of fifth-graders, many children in private school who received more praise and positive statements from their teachers, peers, and siblings had much higher self-esteem and higher rates of positive self-talk habits compared to public school students [4].

This study does not mean that you must go to a private school as a child to develop positive self-talk. Rather, it illustrates the effect that positive statements and praise can have on children and their self-esteem and self-talk. Children in private schools happen to receive more positive statements and praise, but a public school student who receives lots of encouragement can also develop high self-esteem and positive self-talk habits. It all starts in childhood.

Parents and teachers shape your mind when you are young; you look to them to model how the world is and how you should act [5]. If you are always hearing negative statements and criticism, you begin to believe that these words are true. As you grow older, you fear that other people will find out what a "failure" you are and confirm the negative statements that you heard throughout your life. Thus, you criticize yourself harshly, hang back in fear, and drive yourself crazy trying to be perfect in order to avoid hearing more hurtful statements [5].

But there may be a genetic predisposition to it, as well. If you have a genetic propensity for depression, anxiety, or other such mental disorders, then your mind is already "set up" for negative self-talk [6]. This hardly means that you can't change the behavior. It just means that you will tend to engage in self-talk despite having a positive upbringing and a good life, and this thinking habit is not a product of environment. With some habit-forming work, you can still address and change your self-talk to be more positive.

Negative life events can make negative self-talk appear [7]. A loss of a loved one is a major tragic event that can crumple your self-esteem and happiness. Rejections or difficult circumstances, like divorce, job termination, chronic illness, and bankruptcy, can also have this effect. Any traumatic experience, such as being the victim of a violent crime or abuse, witnessing a violent crime, surviving a catastrophe, or serving in a war, can further weaken your resolve to be happy, since you have seen the dark side of life. You may feel guilty for some perceived responsibility or fault in the event, which corrodes your self-esteem. You may have been manipulated by a person to believe that you deserved what has happened to you. No matter what happened, a bad experience or repeated bad experiences can muddy your positivity and make you take a gloomy outlook on life or even engage in self-loathing. Counseling and engaging in positive self-talk by choice can help you overcome the pain of these events.

Furthermore, social isolation can magnify negative

self-talk [8]. Without positive influences to check your thinking, you don't have anyone to lift you up from dark or self-defeating thoughts. The sense that you are alone and that something must be wrong with you to keep you so isolated can further add to the gloom in your mind. You will notice that your mood can darken the more time you spend by yourself. Being social can certainly improve your self-talk.

The Consequences Of Negative Self-Talk

Now let's discuss why fixing negative self-talk is so essential. The consequences of negative self-talk are very real and very detrimental. Negative self-talk can corrode away your quality of life over time. Correcting it is imperative to maintaining happiness and good health.

Psychologists understand the fact that negative self-talk can harm you so well that they have dedicated a massive amount of time and research to developing cognitive behavioral therapies that rectify your narrative [9]. Various techniques have been established to help turn negative self-talk to positive self-talk. Athletes and businessmen are often taught these techniques because they are so effective in reversing negative self-talk and thus improving performance. These techniques are presented in the following pages, but first, learn why they are so important to use.

The voice in your head drags you down mentally, emotionally, spiritually, and physically. It negatively impacts your ability to be your best. As you repeatedly tell yourself that you aren't worthy or you can't do something, you begin to believe it. Then you waste potential because you don't even try. You hurt yourself repeatedly with these statements, which lowers your mood. You naturally fall into a pit of despair and self-loathing.

The first and foremost disastrous consequence of

negative self-talk is low self-esteem. If you are constantly berating yourself mentally, you are not saying anything nice to build yourself up. The result is that you start to focus only on your flaws, which makes you hate yourself. As your self-esteem dwindles, so does your mental health. Low self-esteem has been linked to the gradual development of severe mental illness, ranging from depression to social anxiety to panic disorder [10]. One's self-esteem is considered the single most important aspect of mental and physical health, in fact [10].

This mental despair can spill into your physical health. There is a proven link between your health and your mental outlook. People with depression tend to have more physical health issues than those without depression [11]. In some cases, having a chronic illness can cause the despair and hopelessness that characterizes depression; but depression itself can also cause one to neglect his or her health and can lead to physical symptoms that cause health issues, such as overeating, ulcers caused by stress, sleep deprivation or oversleeping, lack of social activity, and lack of exercise [11].

Negative self-talk can also lead to sleep deprivation. As you stay up all night ruminating on what a bad person you are and how much you have ruined your life, you generate a massive amount of stress [2]. Depression tends to alter your melatonin production and increases cortisol production, which can keep you up at night [11]. Then your body is not able to heal from regular illnesses or injuries. You can experience weight gain, which comes with its own host of health problems. Furthermore, your concentration and mental clarity suffer, affecting your performance at work and in life in general. You can experience irritability and impulsive decision-making.

Not to mention how your social life will change for the worse. If you are always down in the dumps, people don't think that you are fun to be around. You may also neglect or avoid social functions because you are scared of being criticized. As you neglect your social life, you tend to withdraw into social isolation, which only worsens negative self-talk and depression [8].

As you can see, each of the problems caused by negative self-talk tends to also exacerbate negative self-talk. So, as you engage in negative self-talk, your mind enters a vicious spiral that only drags you down further. The only way to change your life around and see improvement is to cut down on negative self-talk.

Chapter 2: Turning Back To Positive Self-Talk

Previously we covered why negative self-talk is bad. But now let's focus a bit on why positive self-talk is so good. Decades of scientific research has led to the realization that positive self-talk has numerous benefits for your life.

Benefits Of Positive Self-Talk

Most research has pointed to great benefits from positive self-talk. After some contradictory results from a 1980 study that failed to show any difference between elite skiers' performance and self-talk, Raalte and some other researchers decided to conduct a study of their own regarding self-talk and its effects on dart players to settle the debate once and for all.

They found that dart players who practiced positive self-talk before a game played better [12]. They generally had more confidence and higher scores.

Players who engaged in negative self-talk had the opposite results. This study is largely what fueled the major trend of encouraging athletes to use positive self-talk before a big competition.

Nevertheless, this doesn't just apply to athletes or dart players. Positive self-talk can ease anxiety and heighten performance in anyone. It is useful before any big event that you feel nervous about. Talking yourself up before a big test, a job interview, a presentation at work, or asking someone out on a date can be beneficial. It can lead to success and victory on your part.

Positive self-talk has been indicated in several benefits [13]. Mainly, this form of self-talk can reduce anxiety. People who are less anxious tend to be more confident and take more action in life. Thus, positive self-talk can make you bolder and readier to take on new opportunities. It can reduce anxious thoughts, panic attacks, and social anxiety as well.

It also enhances self-confidence [12]. This is because it increases your belief in yourself and your love for yourself. As you talk yourself up, you believe what you tell yourself. It is true that we tend to believe what we think. Therefore, positive self-talk can help you feel at one with yourself and reduce the doubt and lack of confidence that can be so debilitating. Furthermore, confidence has been indicated to be more attractive to other people, so being confident can make you more popular [13].

Being more popular has the effect of also growing your confidence even more. As people praise you and give you good feedback, you begin to believe it. You begin to adopt the attitude that you are a likable person. Earning the approval of others starts with positive self-talk. This can make relationships healthier and more possible.

Positive self-talk also increases performance and effort

[12]. If you give yourself a boost with positive self-talk, you tend to try harder. This may be because you actually believe you can do it and you want to prove to yourself that you can be successful. It may also relate to increased confidence and decreased anxiety. To make the most out of an event or perform at your best, use positive self-talk for motivation.

Needless to say, if you use positive self-talk and stop negative thoughts in their tracks, you can rework your mind to eliminate negative self-talk over time. Then you will counter the negative, toxic effects of negative self-talk. Depression, anxiety, and stress can all disappear with the use of positive self-talk. Be sure to practice it regularly to make it a habit.

Raalte observed other studies and found that positive self-talk by itself is not that useful. This is because you can undercut positive thoughts with negative ones. The true success of positive self-talk comes when you actively restructure your mind to no longer entertain negative self-talk. Thought stopping and cognitive restructuring were found to be the best ways to accomplish this [12]. Cognitive or dialectic behavioral therapy can be useful in teaching yourself to practice positive self-talk all of the time.

The dart players did not get a jolt just from thinking, "I can play really well today!" The ones who succeeded usually practiced positive self-talk in their daily lives. This positive self-talk was a habit for them. Meanwhile, the negative self-talk players who did not play as well generally engaged in negative self-talk in their daily lives. Thus, to really reap the benefits of positive self-talk, you must work to make it a daily habit. Only then will it fuel the changes you wish to see in your demeanor and overall life.

What Positive Self-Talk Is Like

Positive self-talk is much like conversing with a best friend who is struggling with something. When you engage in negative self-talk, you harshly criticize and condemn yourself, beating yourself up needlessly. You hurt yourself and don't actually accomplish anything. If anything, you work yourself up so much that you become totally frozen and inactive. Depression, anxiety, and stress-related health problems are thus born.

Would you talk to a friend like this? Chances are, no. You would instead try to praise and comfort your friend to help him or her through the said issue. You would accept his or her faults and imperfections with compassion and try to help him or her feel better.

You won't believe how wonderful it feels to stop beating yourself up. As you enter a new mental outlook on life, you start to feel so much better. You stop driving daggers into your own heart and instead treat yourself with the love and tenderness you would treat your best friend with.

You Will Look Better

As you begin to engage in positive self-talk, it will show in how you carry yourself, how you look, and how you talk and act. You may even dress in a more flattering way to reflect your renewed sense of self-importance and greatness. Other people will notice. Big life changes can start happening pretty rapidly, as people begin to extend opportunities to you and invite you to try new things. Having a good social life is a positive and enriching factor in life itself.

Be ready for people to start smiling at you more. You will generate positivity and cheer, which makes people feel good around you. You will also smile a lot without realizing it, as a reflection of your internal happiness. Other people will respond in kind. The exchange of smiles will only add to your sense of positivity.

You Will Make More Friends

Also, be ready for an influx of friends and new acquaintances. New and positive experiences will come your way as more people enter your life. When you engage in positive self-talk, you speak more positively and take more positive action. People like this and respond to it well. More people will want to spend time around you as you spread around your wonderful attitude.

You will also have the confidence to try new things. You might go to that swing class you always wanted to attend, but never did out of fear that you would look like a clown dancing. You might start attending some sort of group or join a social club. This puts you in contact with more potential friends and grows your network. You can beat social anxiety and work up the courage to go out by talking to yourself positively.

Above all, you will be your own best friend. Out of everyone you meet in life, you are the only one that you are guaranteed to live with for the rest of your life. Hence, if you make it easy and pleasant to live with yourself by taking care of yourself, you will be much happier. You will find that positive self-talk encourages you to like yourself more, take better care of yourself, and treat yourself as a priority. This will make you infinitely happier.

Better Health Comes With Positive Self-Talk

You will feel infinitely better, as you begin to practice positive self-talk. You will notice improvements to your health and your mental well-being as you defeat depression and its debilitating symptoms.

Healthier habits and a sense of accomplishment will also accompany positive self-talk. You no longer feel as stressed, so you won't want to pig out on chips in front of bad TV as much as anymore. You will welcome healthy habits because they make you feel good and your self-talk reminds you that you deserve to feel good.

You will also have fewer urges to engage in unhealthy behavior such as smoking, gambling, or impulse shopping. Often, these bad habits are the result of stress. The brief adrenaline rush that comes with a gambling spree can make you feel better for an instant. Then the reality of what you have just done sets in and you feel even worse. It is a vicious cycle that can drag on for years. Positive self-talk can eliminate the need for these vices.

The reduction in stress that positive self-talk brings can eliminate depression, anxiety, stress-related weight gain, and insomnia. Your mind will be at ease, as well as your body. Say good-bye to frustrating symptoms and bad habits as you enter a new phase of true well-being.

Finances Will Improve

Be prepared for an uptick in your financial success. As you believe in yourself suddenly, you will have the confidence to take on opportunities and make your career happen. The bold career moves that you avoided before because you felt you weren't capable of handling them are now suddenly possible.

With negative self-talk, you might shy away from a lucrative business opportunity. "How can I possibly do that? It's too [insert self-defeating excuse] or I'm too [insert self-insult]." You perpetuate the idea that you can't achieve things. But when you switch that narrative, you start to see that things really are possible. You take charge and do things you never thought possible. Positive self-talk breaks down the barriers that are holding you back.

You might gain the confidence necessary to leave your job and shoot for that dream job or open your own business. Or you might use that new surge of confidence to start a new hobby and make some new friends. Either way, you will welcome and feel ready for new challenges and new opportunities.

Confidence will also increase your problem-solving abilities and your effort. You might perform better at work and bring home a pay raise or bigger commissions. Talk yourself up before you have to do something at work, and see how you perform more awesomely.

You Will Create A Positive Self-Talk Environment

The environment you live in drastically affects your ability to engage in self-talk. If you live in a negative environment, you are always inclined to think negatively. That can spread to your own self-image and treatment of yourself.

Positive self-talk can lead you to love yourself. As a result, you will no longer appreciate people or situations that hurt you. You will start to set up boundaries, defend yourself, and say no when you need to. You will no longer feel a desire to engage with hurtful or negative people who bring you down.

To facilitate positive self-talk, a positive environment is ideal. You want to cut out toxic people and leave a stressful job where your horrible boss calls you names in front of the office. When someone hurts you, stage a healthy confrontation and ask the person to make amends.

Also, do what makes you happy. The happier you are, the more likely you are to engage in positive self-talk. Then positive self-talk will cause you to want to do things you enjoy. It's a self-sustaining cycle.

You Will Be Able To Create A Positive Self-Talk Environment For Others

Often, entire demographics can be hurt by negative self-talk. Kids growing up in a disenfranchised and impoverished area will often hear how life is unfair and the world is turned against them from their families. They grow up believing this and don't try because they think there is no use. A few manage to turn this self-talk around and enjoy considerable success, however. You hear stories every day about kids who grew up in the "ghetto" but went on to have amazing careers.

Oprah Winfrey is a shining example.

Positive self-talk is important for teachers and parents to show their students [2]. Significant others should also show this to their partners. By modeling positive self-talk, you can create a habit in your child. Speak to your child nicely. Use constructive criticism. For instance, when your child does something wrong, you can gently tell him or her how to do it instead of yelling, "You always mess things up!"

Furthermore, you can set a model by always speaking to yourself and about yourself nicely. You are not setting a good model by berating yourself when you get into a car accident. Saying things like, "I'm so stupid" or "I always mess things up" teach your children to say this to themselves as well. Being kind to yourself, encouraging yourself, and refusing to talk badly about yourself denotes a massive amount of self-respect and self-love. Children will learn from this model and act the same way themselves.

An environment created around positive self-talk is warm and encouraging. You compliment people and tell them what they do best. You highlight their strengths and talents. You also do this to yourself, and you receive ample praise and encouragement back.

Think of a good home, where loving parents dote on their children. You don't hear a lot of cussing, name calling, or berating in this environment.

Think of a sports team, where all of the members build each other up. After a game, you hear the team members congratulate each other. They may offer suggestions for improvements, but they don't tear each other down or scream at each other. They also don't stand there criticizing themselves.

These are examples of positive environments. Focus on building such environments to influence those around you. In turn, you will influence yourself to take on this new approach to self-talk. Always set a model for others and you will receive benefits too.

By setting a model, you not only spread the habit of positive self-talk to children or other people around you, but you also have a reason to engage in positive self-talk. This can make the habit easier to develop because you have a good source of motivation.

How To Initiate Change

Now you see clearly how positive self-talk is the greatest invention since sliced bread! But that's not enough to make you change. There is more to it, which you will learn in this book.

Change is not easy for anyone. People tend to settle into habits, including bad ones, and then encounter difficulties changing them because they are comfortable. Even if your thinking habits cause you considerable suffering, you are still comfortable engaging in these habits because you have done so for a long time [14].

The science of habit-formation indicates that habits are formed in one of two ways: System 1 or System 2 [14]. System 2, the most common *and* unsuccessful form of habit change, involves hearing "You need to change your negative thinking because it's bad for you!" You imagine how much better your life is going to be as long as you change, and then you decide to change and put all of your energy behind it. When you don't see results immediately, your motivation and attention wane, making you lose sight of your goals and let your new positive thinking habits fall to the wayside. You try to force a new habit and it just doesn't work.

The truth is that changing a habit takes a lot of action and correction. Habits are automatic responses to stimulus [14]. Your brain saves time by automating its response so that you don't have to spend too much thinking, "What should I do now?" To correct your thinking, you must recognize your automatic habit of thinking negatively and then retrain your brain to automate positive thinking instead.

To successfully shape new habits, you must engage in a System 1 habit formation plan, which automates habits. This basically involves repeating a habit every day for 66 days without scanning too hard for results. At that point, automation takes over and you don't have to keep up the rigorous work [14]. Abandon the pressure of System 2 and simply use a reminder to engage in your habit once a day, 66 days in a row, and then your brain takes over for you. The results sneak up on you.

Another important aspect of System 1 habit formation is making the change easy, so you don't have to put in as much effort [14]. Work around your schedule. Write in your thought journal at a convenient moment for you, such as before bed, to take the stress out of clearing a patch in your schedule and dredging up the motivation to work on your habit.

Also, find a contextual clue to trigger your automatic reaction, so your brain never forgets to trigger its habitual response. Most of us wash our hands (habit) after using the bathroom (contextual clue). To find a contextual clue relevant to thinking, determine times when you are especially hard on yourself. This might be when you reflect on the day as you lie in bed, or when you submit a project to your boss at work, or when you have a confrontation. These times become your contextual cues. When the cue happens, you then know to activate your new positive self-talk habit to override the inevitable negative self-talk habit. Basically, you don't have to remind yourself to work on your self-talk anymore because you have chosen key times when you must work on it. Working on positive self-talk every time you get the cue and negative self-talk starts running in your head makes it an automatic habit with time.

How To Start Using System 1

The first step is to realize that you have a problem with negative self-talk. You have probably already completed this step since you are reading this book. The next step is to define the problem in simple words that your brain can clearly understand: "I use negative self-talk which damages my self-esteem and leads to other life problems." Write that statement down to cement it in your brain.

From there, you can start identifying the moments you have negative self-talk. In a journal, document the moments that you think negatively and the words you say to yourself. You might not be able to catch every single negative thought, but you can catch the main big ones.

Now, decide on helpful replacement thoughts. These are positive thoughts that should take the place of negative ones in your mind. For instance, if you forgot to buy bread on a grocery store run, your habit may be to tell yourself, "I forgot the bread! I'm such an idiot. I forget everything." A more helpful positive thought is something like, "Oops, I forgot the bread. It's OK because everyone forgets things now and then. I had better go back to get more bread."

The thoughts that kick you down a notch and make you feel bad need to go. For each of these thoughts, there is a subsequent positive one that you can use instead to uplift yourself and find a solution to a problem in your life. Find the contextual cues when your ugly thoughts start running amok in your mind, and then work on thinking about the replacement thoughts, even writing them down or reciting them out loud.

Also, take a moment to reflect on your motivation each day. Write down a statement about why you want to change your thinking. This helps cement System 1 habit formation by keeping you invested in your new endeavor.

As you begin to plan how to talk to yourself, you are in a good place to start implementing the techniques in the next chapter. You already know the problem and how you want to change. Now you just need to know the methods and how to build motivation.

Chapter 3: The Secrets To Positive Self-Talk

To begin using positive self-talk and eradicating negative self-talk, there are several things you can do. These activities will change your thinking and your approach to situations in life. With time and practice, they become habitual routine, so you start to use positive self-talk regularly.

In addition, using positive self-talk and different methods to attain that attitude will show you how great it can be. Thus, you feel more motivated to use it more often. Experience can be an excellent motivator. These techniques help you change your thinking so that you see quick results and experience rapid relief. Then, you can start to implement them in your daily life when you realize how wonderful they are for your mental and physical health.

Self-Distance

It is possible to put distance between yourself and a situation to think about it objectively [3]. Think of how someone else might see you. If you think, "Another person would see me as an abject failure," then think of how you could change your behavior so that someone would see you as a success.

Self-distance is a great way to remove the emotion from a thought process and make a logical decision that is ideal for your situation [3]. It can also help you determine the necessary actions to actually affect change in your life. Just talking to yourself positively is a helpful action, but it's not enough to make a real difference. The difference starts when you use self-talk to drive positive action and positive decisions in your life.

By putting self-distance in place, you can focus more on finding a solution to a problem that is troubling you. When you are looking at life from inside of your own lens, you only see the limitations and hurdles that you have erected around yourself. It is thus easy to get lost in despair and give up. By removing these lenses and thinking, "What is best for this person?", as if evaluating yourself from someone else's standpoint, it becomes more obvious what you must do. Then you can objectively address the limitations and hurdles, removing them without dwelling on the pain and frustration they cause you.

I'll never forget the day I decided to go back to college. For years, I had worked dead-end jobs and thought, "I can't possibly afford to go back to college." I would read cool job postings, then see the requirement for a bachelor's or higher and abandon the posting, thinking, "Good jobs just aren't for me." One day, I thought, "I obviously want to go to college and I need to. The best decision, to make me a person that I'm proud of, is to go back. So, let's see how to make this possible." From there, I made a series of good decisions that helped me get back on track: I sought the help of an academic advisor to align myself with my desired degree, I looked into financial aid, I took a few community college classes to prepare for my degree at my state university, and I ultimately graduated into a new life.

Another example is Lebron James [3]. When choosing between staying with his small-market team for nostalgic reasons or moving to a larger team which scared him, he was torn by emotion which removed his ability to reason. Then he decided to remove the emotion from the equation by putting self-distance in place and asking himself, "What would make Lebron James happy?" The answer thus became clear to him: Go to the larger team. Now he is a famous basketball player featured in the Basketball Hall of Fame. He probably never would have made it so far had he not made this huge life decision using self-distance.

Utilize Self-Talk

At times, negative self-talk can be a useful tool for

elevating yourself to a better position or for driving better performance. For instance, if you perform some sloppy work and you know it, you can direct yourself to improve the work into something great that you are proud of.

Being able to criticize yourself can be useful, as long as you use that criticism to better yourself. All humans have a built-in self-critic. This self-critic regulates your behavior through language [3]. The problem lies in letting this self-critic tell you that you can't do something or you are not good enough.

There is nothing wrong with listening to your self-critic, as long as you use it as a motivational tool to make improvements. Always focus on solutions to the flaws you see in your performance. You don't want to just dwell on the fact that you are imperfect, as that doesn't help anything or anyone at all. Instead, think, "I don't like what I just did. How can I make it better? How can I get the results I want?"

It is unrealistic to expect to be happy all of the time, or to expect yourself to always be perfect. Accepting the fact that you are imperfect opens your eyes to ways to improve upon your imperfections for better outcomes. Noticing that something is wrong in your work, your marriage, your friendship, your habits, or your personality enables you to make beneficial changes. Being blind to problems in life only prevents you from handling them.

Therefore, negative self-talk is not always the enemy. Allow this self-talk to arise at times and listen to it. Harness the insight you gain from it by chasing every negative thought with, "Is this something I really need to address?" If the self-talk is pointing out a very real problem that can decline the quality of your life in some way, then you should address it.

The next thought to chase the first one with is, "How can I go about fixing this?" When you make negative self-talk a source of inspiration for recognizing and solving a problem, it immediately becomes a very positive tool in your self-toolbox.

Let's say you are used to beating yourself up for being fat. That is not good because you are only hurting your mental health and causing stress with these thoughts. The stress can lead to you eating more as a source of comfort, so you only gain more weight. To beat out of this cycle, listen to yourself the next time you think bitterly, "I'm such a whale." Then, think, "I hate being a whale because of how people look at me and how I am hurting my health. My quality of life is suffering because of my weight." From there, ask yourself, "What can I do about my weight to stop feeling so bad about myself and hurting myself? How can I fix my weight-related problems?" Use the pain you feel as being overweight to drive your desire to lose it and get healthy and fit.

"Fat talk" is a perfect example of harmful negative self-talk at play. People who hear fat talk in the media or from friends internalize it and begin to think that it is true. They then suffer from a sharp decline in body image satisfaction, which can lead to depression, overeating, or eating disorders [15]. Yet people who enjoyed successful weight loss were able to use fat talk to their advantage. They let the pain and dissatisfaction motivate them to lose weight.

Hence, there is no reason to beat yourself up if you still use negative self-talk from time to time. Talking to yourself negatively because you are talking to yourself negatively is pretty silly. Instead, use this habit constructively. Gain some good out of it. Then, you will reap more benefits than if you simply try to force yourself to be positive all of the time.

Importance Of Repeating

In order to make positive self-talk a habit, you must make non-negativity a habit. The best way to do this is to use repetition [14]. Repetition will drill messages into your head and provide you with a clear idea of what you need to do.

To start using positive self-talk, you must repeat positive messages. You can do this after you think a negative thought by forcing yourself to think a positive one. Chase negative thoughts with positive ones. Another way is to think positively at certain times throughout the day, repeating mantras by rote. Read on to the part about mantras to learn how to do this.

Here's an example. You hit the curb. Your impulse in this stressful moment is to think, "You dummy!" You may yell it out loud or yell it in your head, but the negative message is obvious and hateful toward yourself. Then you chase that thought with another one: "I need to pay more attention. I'm actually a good driver."

Doing this often can drill the habit of positive self-talk

into your head and show you how to talk to yourself more positively. Try a little positive self-talk every day, even if you have to force it, and you will notice it becomes easier and easier. Pretty soon, you won't need to force it anymore.

Here is why repetition works. Many people think that habits are formed by reward. If you work out and see how good you feel after, you are more likely to keep working out. But anyone who has struggled with getting in enough gym time understands that habit formation doesn't work like that. A study suggests that habits are formed through repetition, *not* reward [16].

This study compared people who strove to form habits by receiving rewards and those who formed habits through repetition. Guess who actually formed habits? The ones who used repetition [16]. The result is clear, that repetition will rewire your brain to be more positive than simply focusing on the rewards of thinking positively.

People don't form habits based on the outcomes of their behavior. This is why the horrible habit of negative self-talk sticks, because your brain doesn't focus on the negative outcomes. This is why people get "addicted" to things despite outrageously bad outcomes – they don't learn from outcomes, but rather from the actions they have already performed.

Rather, the brain builds habits based on recently performed actions. So, to change your habits, you must perform the actions of positive self-talk [16]. Only then will your brain start to make positive self-talk a habit. It won't care about how great positive self-talk is or how you really should do it; the brain is somehow impervious to learning by outcomes, as much as we would like to think otherwise.

But how much repetition is necessary? As discussed under System 1, it can take 66 days to form a habit. Practicing positive thinking and positive self-talk in some manner for 66 days should provide sufficient repetition to make the habit stick.

Using these study results constructively, you now know to perform positive self-talk every day for 66 days. But you should also drive home the habit of stopping negative thoughts or using negative thoughts constructively. That will also become a good habit that reinforces your new habit of positive self-talk. Positive self-talk can only occur in a vacuum where negative self-talk does not exist. Learning how to stop negative self-talk *and* engage in positive self-talk is a two-fold habit formation process that can be accomplished through rote.

The Reprogramming Process

Computers were modeled after the actual human brain. Thus, the brain works a lot like a computer and you have more control over it than you think. It is actually possible to reprogram your mind, just as you would reprogram software or install a whole new operating system on your computer.

Reprogramming is the simple act of taking your thoughts and directing them to behave differently. Gain a clear idea of what you want your new mind to be like. Think about how you want to use more positive self-talk in your thinking. Then, capture your negative thoughts and make them do what you want.

Ultimately, this process lets you gain victory over the most elusive and rebellious part of your body: your mind. You might think, "I have all sorts of renegade thoughts! I can't control what I'm thinking! What are you talking about, taking my thoughts captive and changing them?" But this process is more than possible. Reprogramming is a step-by-step process that may take some time to become a habit.

Reprogramming is possible because of neuroplasticity [17]. This is your brain's ability to learn things and then form new neural pathways to accommodate the new information and a subsequent appropriate reaction. For instance, you were probably a naïve youth once, and then you got your heart broken for the first time. Your brain never knew betrayal and heartbreak of the romantic sort before, so when it encountered it, it reprogramed itself to accommodate trust issues and a fear of abandonment in an effort to avoid being hurt again. Fortunately, just as the brain can reprogram itself negatively, it can also reprogram itself more positively to get over such learning behaviors as trust issues or, of course, negative self-talk.

Dr. John Demartini is a leader in mental reprogramming using neuroplasticity. He uses a technique where he neutralizes the fear and aggression of the amygdala by having someone think about the good that comes from a bad situation [17]. This makes the brain start to think differently and form new neural pathways in response to the situation that causes it so much pain.

For instance, maybe your parent abandoned you when you were little and you now have a propensity for negative self-talk, rooted in the belief that you are not good enough which is why your parent left. By thinking about that horrible experience made you a strong person more than capable of surviving on his or her own, you start to reprogram your thoughts about the abandonment. You make your brain stop resorting to its old path of thought: "I am not good enough." You instead think, "I am a strong person." The result is that you eliminate a lot of dark thoughts about yourself and a lot of negative self-talk just be reframing your perspective on the situation.

Tony Robbins also offers a method of reprogramming that combines physical movement with new feelings [18]. Called priming, Robbins suggests this method to prime your brain to feel something different. When you are feeling negative, sit in a chair, and close your eyes. Raise your fists and then breathe out through your nose, lowering your fists. Do this thirty times.

Focusing on this behavior raises your heart rate while clearing your head. Then you feel neutral. You are able to flood yourself with love and gratitude, which can make your brain take a different neural route than its usual one of anger, bitterness, or anxiety.

Robbins recommends starting the day with this so that you are able to neutralize emotions and then make them positive throughout the next twenty-four hours. But you can also use priming whenever you feel the negative self-talk build up to a fever pitch in your mind. Either way, you can reprogram your mind's response to things using priming.

Furthermore, affirmations and visualizations are incredibly effective methods of reprogramming. I cover them shortly. Pairing them with these methods when you start to think negatively will have a similar effect on your thinking.

When the negative self-talk starts, actively try to

reprogram your mind by priming yourself with Robbins' method. As you feel better after, you can start to look at your situation differently by asking a series of questions that lead to positive thinking, through Demartini's method. The two methods combined can have a really positive effect on your overall thinking. They can train your brain to focus on the positive and to stop harboring negative emotion.

When you think about an upsetting memory, you are really remembering the last time you remembered it. Usually, the last time you remembered it, you felt negative. But once you use one or both of these reprogramming methods, you think about it positively for once. The next time the memory comes up, you thus remember it in the positive way you did during the reprogramming session. This creates a habit and completely restructures how your brain handles the memory.

Sometimes, people want to hold onto anger. Anger

fuels them more than sadness and feels more proactive, even though it really is not. Thus, it may be hard for you to want to reprogram your brain. It feels better to cling to grudges or "comfortable" negative thinking.

You may also find it difficult to face a memory or find anything good about something bad that happened to you. As long as you attempt it, you can begin the reprogramming process that can eradicate the negative views you have about yourself based on past abuse, abandonment, or trauma. Chances are, your negative self-talk is rooted in some negative self-belief fueled by an unkind memory, such as a parents' criticism or some horrible event from your past.

If you find it too difficult to do this on your own, therapy can help. A hypnotherapist or psychologist who specializes in EMDR can reprogram your brain through questions, affirmations, and repetitive movements. They can help you feel less alone as you revisit extremely troubling traumas. They can also point out a silver lining if you can't see one yourself. Having a trained outside perspective when dealing with brain reprogramming can be extremely helpful.

Importance Of Visualization

Neurolinguistic programming, or NLP, teaches you to change your modality to reprogram your own brain [19]. Your modality is simply how you see and understand the world inside your mind. People operate on different modalities, but all modalities are based on the same principle: They are a way for your brain to process the information it takes in from the world in a simplified way using one of the main senses: sight, sound, taste, smell, or touch [19]. Most people use sight or sound as their primary modality [19].

Negative self-talk is an example of an auditory modality. You are processing the world around you and instructing yourself how to respond to life events or situations with verbal cues. You are "hearing" the voice inside your head, or in other words, you are hearing yourself think.

To use visualizations to change negative self-talk, you must change your auditory modality to a visual one. This makes the negative self-talk irrelevant. It can be pretty difficult to scold yourself or call yourself an idiot with an image. If you do, the image will probably be pretty silly and make you laugh, which lessens the negativity of the situation.

Processing the world in a more visual way can help you step back. It can help you "see" things more clearly. But mostly, it just removes all of the verbal garbage that you are abusing yourself with. Instead of focusing on calling yourself a dummy or a failure, you can focus on how the situation looks right now and how you want it to look.

Furthermore, visualizations can act as distractions. You essentially remove yourself from the equation as you focus your energy on imagining some sort of complex image. Guided meditations help you relax by channeling your energy into visualizing a peaceful forest, for instance. By using a visualization technique, you can stop thinking about your negative self-image and distract yourself to something more pleasing. Then, you can return to problem-solving mode in a more relaxed mood, and you can approach finding a solution without abusing yourself.

A powerful visualization will first feature something that calms you down. Perhaps imagine a nice beach setting or a forest where you can only hear the wind in the leaves and the birds chirping. As you settle your nerves, you can move on to the next part.

The next part must feature your problem or your feelings. You must visualize them in a lifelike form. For instance, maybe you are beating yourself up for displeasing your boss, who always calls you a useless idiot. You can reduce your boss to a yammering cartoon to make him appear both smaller and less intimidating than you are making him out to be.

The third part involves visualizing how you vanquish this problem. This part teaches your brain that your problems are surmountable. Something can be done, and you can do it. This gives your brain confidence to tackle the problem in real life.

The final part involves picturing yourself as the victor. You want to create an image of yourself that helps you feel good. Being that victorious knight in shining armor, or that beautiful princess who just fought off an army, can make you feel better about yourself. It can also show your brain how you *could* be if you handled your problem with an effective solution.

Visualizations work in these four parts because they illustrate something to your brain. They send an actual message that alters your brain's perception of reality. As you sit ruminating on a problem and speaking to yourself vulgarly, you are engaging in a limited aspect, where your brain magnifies the problem. The visualization shows your brain that it is more than possible to view this problem differently, to stop making it so huge, and to deal with it effectively so that you emerge victoriously.

Let's look at the actual science behind visualizations. How do they actually work? Several studies have shown that the brain processes visualizations, or imagined scenarios, the exact same way as real scenarios [20]. Hence, there is really no difference between what you actually see and what you imagine. Your brain treats both as reality and remembers both. So when you visualize something in relation to a real-life troubling situation, your brain responds to the visualization like it's really happening.

It has been found that visualizing a routine is the same as practicing it in real life [20]. Thus, if you have a big dance recital coming up, you can visualize it when you're not practicing and that just helps you practice yet more. The same logic applies to restructuring your self-talk. If you visualize handling your problems in the right way and talking to yourself nicely, it is just as effective as doing it in real life. Your brain considers it valuable practice and absorbs it, making your visualized work part of its reality.

When you start to engage in negative self-talk, take a moment to visualize something that increases your positivity. That way, your brain is focused on a more positive emotion or action. That helps you speak to yourself more kindly. There are many visualization methods that you can employ, but you must ensure that they reframe you in a more positive light. The result is that you reprogram your brain to view you in a more positive light. That eliminates unpleasant self-talk.

Imagine that you feel bad after your boss chews you out. As you sit at your desk, you start to beat yourself up and tell yourself the things your boss just said. You start to believe the worst about yourself. Then you take a step back and visualize yourself in a better light, as the conqueror of your life. When you come back to reality, you believe that you are better than what your boss said, and you are full of confidence to prove it to your boss.

How Do You Visualize?

Your brain is your kingdom. You can do anything you want to do with your visualizations. Find something that works for you by imagining different scenarios that involve the four parts discussed above: relaxing pleasantly, encountering your problems in a smaller form, vanquishing your problems, and emerging as the victor. You may also download a guided visualization app or look one up online and follow it. Whatever brings you relief, quiets the negative self-talk, and encourages you to move forward is great.

For example, I will share what I like to visualize.

1. I picture myself in a plain or meadow at dusk, wearing armor and wielding a magical butterfly sword. This image is beautiful and powerful and it relaxes me.

2. I start to walk through the meadow, taking in how beautiful it is. I take in the setting sun and the wildflowers. Maybe I see a rainbow. I can feel the ground under my feet as I walk, and I can smell the fresh air. This relaxes me yet more as I stop focusing on my problems and instead focus on the construction of a beautiful fantasy world.

3. I then gather up my imaginary army of squirrels, foxes, and rainbow zebras that make me feel safe. I now have allies and I am not alone in the world. That is a comforting thought.

4. Next, I encounter my thoughts. I visualize the terrible thoughts as having physical forms. They take the shapes of ugly trolls, warty dwarves, and evil serpents. Each thing that is bringing me down

gets an image that is equivalent to its severity and magnitude in my life.

5. I take my army and go in for the kill. With my sword, I slash down my enemies and then they disappear with a satisfying popping sound. I also picture my army fighting with me, taking out enemies that are too strong for me. No one enemy is left standing.

6. I hold up my sword, which is dripping with blood, and yell, "I am the victor!" I imagine the sunset lighting up my armor, which doesn't even have a dent. The wind streams my hair behind me as I raise my chest. I feel truly strong and wonderful in this visualization.

Here is another one I like to use when I am dealing with hurtful things I say to myself. I imagine what I have to say to myself, as if someone else is saying it to me, and I let it hurt me. I acknowledge the pain as a stab wound. Then I picture the person's voice turning into a cartoon voice that makes me laugh. I picture it getting sillier and sillier, and quieter and quieter, until it fades away. The stab wound feeling is now gone. The words I have said to myself are now gone too, and they don't mean anything. They are just words. I can now move on.

I may also visualize a person who has hurt me. I visualize the person's face in front of me in color. I let the person speak, hearing their words in my mind. Then I mute the picture, as if it were a TV. I switch it to black and white. I turn it into a black and white cartoon or slapstick, like something from the 1950s, so that it seems silly. This helps me take it less seriously. After that, I start shrinking the frame of the TV picture until it is so small that I can't see it. Now, this person is gone; I can't see or hear what he or she said. And I have not allowed myself to engage in belittling self-talk in relation to the person's words. I certainly didn't internalize their words as the truth about myself. They are just a little voice that has disappeared from my mind and they are no longer relevant!

When I am stressed, I tend to use more negative self-talk. I defeat myself by thinking that I can't handle the situation at hand because I'm too overwhelmed. That is when I visualize myself walking along a peaceful beach, listening to the waves lapping at my feet, hearing the seagulls spiraling over my head. As a result, I instantly feel more serene. My brain believes the stress is gone and stops reacting to it. When I come back to reality, I am in a better place to handle my business because I no longer feel stressed.

Visualizations also work well with traumatic memories. When you start to have a flashback to a bad memory, you can take control of it. Tell yourself, "I want it to end differently now." Visualize a totally different set of events and outcome. Imagine what you could have done differently and do it in your mind. Emphasize your sense of righteousness and victory at the end. This helps you reprogram the memory, so that it no longer troubles you as much. It makes your brain believe that you are not weak and powerless and you can do something about the events that hurt or trouble you.

You can download a guided meditation or watch one on Youtube. You can also invent your own visualizations. The key is to force yourself into a new emotional state that gets rid of the trouble and torment of whatever you are dealing with. From that positive space, you can build yourself up. Your brain learns from this as if it's real life and takes a new approach to situations as a result.

The Power Of Mantras

The power of reciting mantras to yourself cannot be understated. Truthfully, mantras are a great way to teach your brain something useful. By repeating a sound or Sanskrit phrase over and over, you make its message clear to yourself. Your brain absorbs it and pays attention to it.

People use mantras to drive life change. The massive

power of mantras has been realized and recognized by many. That's why mantras are a go-to method for many people who are trying to change themselves. They are also a cornerstone in Buddhist meditation, which says something about their ability to change the mind.

The same science that lies behind repetition and visualization also lies behind mantras. Mantras use an auditory modality because you are speaking to yourself. They use repetition to make your brain remember and understand their message. Finally, they use the power of visualization to make your brain adopt them as fact.

A mantra is something short and easy to remember. The catchier or snappier it is, the more your brain will retain it. Think of how you easily remember little commercial slogans or jingles and apply that to your mantras. A simple sentence or sentence fragment is ideal; your brain will be less likely to retain a huge, flowery sentence. You may also use a basic sound that intones a specific meaning for you, or a word in another language that captures the essence of what you are trying to say.

When you repeat the mantra, close your eyes and really focus on what it means for you. Then repeat it over and over. Let the feeling it is supposed to bring you overtake your body.

That conditions your brain to associate the mantra with a particular state. When you use the mantra in the future, your brain automatically recalls the state it is supposed to be in. The association is strong but may need to be renewed. Be sure to set aside some time for meditation where you focus on the mantra and the feeling you want it to symbolize. That keeps the association strong and enduring.

An example of a mantra is the meditation "Om." When you say "Om," you immediately recall the feeling of being calm, collected, and centered in meditation. Even if you can't meditate and reach that particular feeling in a moment, you can still say "Om" and your brain makes you feel that way. This gives you power over yourself and your situation by letting you control your emotional state.

Find a mantra that means a lot to you. Then repeat it when you need it. You can make one up, or use a popular meditation mantra. You can even use a simple phrase in English or imagine an image, such as a lotus flower. Use the mantra a few times in meditation to condition your brain to it and then use it when you need it throughout the hustle and bustle of your daily life.

Positive Affirmations

Positive affirmations work in the same way as mantras. In fact, they are practically the same thing. The main difference is that mantras can simply be sounds you use to gain a certain feeling, while affirmations are statements that you make as truth. As you recite affirmations to yourself, you come to believe them.

Positive affirmations are auditory modalities when you speak them out loud to yourself. They can become visual if you write them or use them in a picture. You can find thousands of positive affirmations online, complete with pictures that reinforce their power.

As you say an affirmation, you start to believe it with repetition. However, you also invoke a feeling with it. It works just like a mantra in this way.

You can have more than one affirmation that you use throughout the day, but one affirmation that drives home the thinking you really want to work on the most is sufficient. Designate an affirmation for each negative self-talk-triggering situation you struggle with. Also, find one that illustrates the main problem you struggle with each day, such as a self-defeating belief or fear. Recite your main affirmation several times a day. Recite the other affirmations when the situation arises that makes them applicable. Recite them at least three times to make them stick in your brain.

To adopt both visual and auditory modalities and cement affirmations more thoroughly in your brain, you can write them down and place them somewhere that you see often. A Post-It note on your laptop with your favorite affirmation is a great idea. I have my computer background set to a revolving series of positive affirmation quotes that I have found online. Then, read the affirmation and repeat it a few times throughout the day. The use of two modalities makes your brain actually believe the affirmation.

One critical aspect of affirmations is to leave out negative words like "not." Don't say something like, "I'm not a bad person." This affirmation doesn't work because it implies negativity and shifts your focus onto the term *bad person*. It can have its opposite intended effect. Instead, use positive language. "I am a good person" is better than "I'm not a bad person." Frame your affirmations to always say the best about yourself. Leave out the phrases and images that are not so friendly.

One example of a positive affirmation might be: "I am a good person." You can repeat this over and over until you believe it. This unearths the belief lying underneath your negative self-talk that you are not a good person.

Or you could say something like, "I got this." I hear a lot of people tell themselves this short, simple phrase before a big task or overwhelming project. The beauty of it is that it works. It undermines the belief that you can't do something. It assures you that you will tackle whatever big obstacle or undertaking lies before you.

"Not my circus, not my monkeys" is an affirmation I use a lot. I tend to internalize what people say to me, letting their words define my reality and self-image. The thing is, what other people think of me does not define me. I realize this fact, but my brain has the habit of forgetting it. So, I remind myself of this fact by reciting this little mantra a few times. It tells my brain to let what someone says or does go, because that person is separate from me and his or her drama is not mine.

"Life is good. I have a lot," is another good one to intone gratitude. Many people have a habit of focusing on the bad in life and forgetting the blessings they do have. This can make you turn bitter and dissatisfied. To remind yourself that you have more than you lack, be sure to recite this affirmation more than once a day. Pair it with a gratitude journal, where you reflect on your day and write down three things you have or that you did well.

"I am beautiful, inside and out," is a great affirmation for people struggling with their physical image. It increases body satisfaction and inspires a sense of confidence. When you start to criticize your looks or internalize something mean someone said to you about your appearance, remind yourself of this fact by reciting this affirmation. You may also use this affirmation if you tend to believe that you are not a good person or you are at fault for everything wrong in others' lives.

"I am worthy" or "I deserve this" is a great affirmation. Many of us feel unworthy of the best, of success, or of our dreams. We find something fundamentally inadequate or flawed within ourselves and then use that to justify fear for going after what we want or accepting something wonderful from life. Instead of doing this, ease up on yourself. Say "I am worthy" and think of all of the things you have done to deserve the best in life.

"I am worth more than this" is a good affirmation for those who are tolerating subpar treatment from others. If your significant other or boss is tearing you down, for instance, you can think this. This affirmation helps you realize that you don't deserve to be abused and mistreated in any way. It gives you the strength to remove toxic people from your life and elevate yourself to a happy existence.

"I am strong" can help you in the face of defeating life circumstances. A lot of addicts like to use an affirmation like this when they feel as if they are about to crumble to cravings. You can use it if you feel scared or weak. It will convince your brain that you do have the strength to accomplish anything, from sobriety to handling a big stressful project at work. It also works for grief, as it reminds you that you will survive despite your devastating emotions.

You can find your own affirmations. Whatever gives you the feeling you need to get through a situation that normally hurts you will work. Affirmations are useful as long as you actually repeat them. With time, they become a comforting ritual that really reprograms your brain.

Fight Negative Thoughts with Thought Stopping

It is a paradigm of human nature that the more you try not to think about something, the more you think about it. If you have ever dieted, for instance, you will notice that you think more about food when you try not to.

The same goes for negative thinking. If you try to not think negative thoughts, you will think about them the same amount or even more. Then, you are still in the same boat. Dwelling on negative self-talk or beating yourself up for engaging in it is self-defeating.

Banishing negative thoughts is neither possible nor

helpful. You simply start to overthink about negativity. Therefore, a better approach is to simply stop negative thoughts in their tracks, without dwelling on them too much. Don't give them any of the attention that they don't deserve.

Since you have engaged in negative self-talk for most of your life, it is a habit. You can and will encounter negative self-talk and thoughts throughout your journey into reprograming your brain for positive self-talk. Handling this inevitability the right way will only broaden your success.

Here is the wrong way to handle these thoughts. When a negative thought enters your mind, your habit is to think something else negative. "There I go again, using that negative self-talk!" You begin to beat yourself up for using negative self-talk. That is not helpful at all.

Rather, acknowledge the thought calmly. Think, "That thought was negative. I'd rather not think like that.

How can I reframe this more positively?" That immediately puts your mind on a more positive track, which invites further positivity.

Then stop the thought. Briefly and firmly tell it to stop. Don't entertain it anymore. Start to think something more positive.

Acknowledge thoughts instead of suppressing them or reprimanding yourself for thinking them. Take notice of them. Think about how they are present. Then tell them to stop and calmly think of something else. This is how you "capture" your thoughts and make them obey you. You don't use force; you use calm but deliberate halting and then redirection [21].

Thought stopping is a common practice in cognitive behavioral therapy [21]. CBT encourages you to sit down with a CBT journal (any journal will do) and write down the most common stressful thoughts you suffer from. These might range from "How can I pay all the bills this month?" to "How can I possibly get all this work done?" These thoughts all have a root in a negative self-belief, probably a belief that you are not good enough and not capable of great things.

Next, imagine the thought. Let it fill it with the dread or panic it normally causes you. You know exactly how this thought makes you feel, because you think it often.

Stop the thought by shouting "Stop!" Then close your eyes and think it again. Again shout "Stop!" You will startle yourself out of the thought each time. You just successfully stopped it.

Practice this a few times. Then start whispering "Stop." See the thought become interrupted. Eventually, you can just imagine yourself saying "Stop" and it will work.

Once the thought has been stopped, your mind is

empty. It will struggle to fill the emptiness, and will probably resort to another negative thought by habit. You can retrain it not to, though, by repeatedly thinking a more positive thought.

In the same journal you write the thoughts down in, write accompanying good thoughts. For example, if you think about how you can't make enough money to cover the bills, think, "I'll find a way or I'll cut bills."

Subsequent positive thoughts can't just be empty platitudes like "Everything will be OK." You must actually reassure yourself by finding a potential solution to a worry. Think about how you can solve a problem. Then you prove to yourself that your worries are groundless and that you are capable of achieving success despite the obstacles that you may face in life. This goes miles for boosting your confidence and your ability to believe in yourself.

Some worries are totally groundless, with no solution.

If you constantly worry about getting cancer, for instance, there is little you can do about that besides attempting to live a healthy life. In this case, stop the thoughts and think instead about how healthy you are. "I don't have cancer!" is the ideal chaser to this negative thought.

When you start to berate yourself with negative self-talk, use the same technique. Acknowledge the thought and how awful it makes you feel. This thought has a root and wants to be expressed, so don't suppress it. Then tell the voice to stop. Next, think of something more positive. You might call yourself an idiot. Think about how bad you feel saying that to yourself, say stop in your head, and then think, "I made a mistake. I'm a very intelligent person." Doing this with repetition really helps you master your self-talk and learn to stop it before it runs amok in your head, destroying your self-esteem.

This same process can spill over into your interactions

with others. IF you start to talk badly to someone, you can tell yourself to stop and speak more kindly. If someone speaks badly to you, you can tell them to stop and ask them to speak more gently. Watch how it helps you redefine and strengthen your communication. What goes in your head tends to come out in your actions, so making your mind a more positive place can make your life more positive.

From now on, when a negative thought intrudes on your mind's peace, always use CBT to stop the thought by whispering "Stop." Then follow the thought up with a more positive one.

Mental Decluttering

Many people suffer what is called "monkey mind." This term comes from Siddhartha Buddha, who likened the mind to monkeys swinging from branch to branch. Your mind jumps around like a monkey, seemingly out of your control. Negative thoughts intrude, no matter how much you don't want them. Fear infiltrates your reasoning. A ton of distracting thoughts clutter your mind, causing you to get lost in them, basically paying more attention to the monkeys swinging around than to your actual work at hand.

A few habits tend to drive this monkey mind more than others. Here are the habits that you should avoid to de-clutter your mind and have more control over your thinking.

The first is procrastination. As you put things off, you tend to weaken your ability to succeed. You cause yourself guilt over your lack of productivity and you beat yourself up for not getting ahead in life. The true cause of procrastination is usually fear of failure. But realize that procrastination will cause you to fail far more than trying will. Actually put in some effort and you will see what is possible.

Generalizations are also harmful. They are a listed cognitive distortion in CBT, or in other words, a harmful thought habit that distorts your perception of reality in a bad way [22]. This is where you think "That man hurt me, so all men are bad." Or you think, "I didn't get that job at a design studio so I must be a horrible designer and I won't get any jobs in this field." You take one instance and apply it to every other possibility in life.

Instead of generalizing, recognize that each person and each situation is different. Even if you have tried to get jobs at many studios with poor results, there is always that one that may accept you. Even if you have dated many horrible men, you are learning from them and one day you will be ready for the right man. Don't apply one, or even several, experiences to life in general. Keep trying and addressing each opportunity or situation as something different.

Evaluations are another cognitive distortion where you compare yourself to others, often unfairly [22]. This causes feelings of jealousy and inadequacy that prevent you from ever enjoying your life or feeling proud of who you are. You might evaluate yourself by thinking how someone you know is so much more accomplished at your age.

The truth is, everyone is different and you can't make an evaluation fairly. Your circumstances have led you to where you are. You don't have to be like your accomplished friend. Furthermore, you might not realize what your friend lacks that you have. Your friend's life may look wonderful on the outside, but it may not be so perfect on the inside. You can't make an evaluation because you will never have all of the facts.

Learn to accept yourself for who you are, instead. If you feel that you are lacking something that somebody else has, work for it. But don't let these feelings of lack create a sense of inadequacy within yourself. Otherwise, you will continually feel defeated and useless or unaccomplished.

Presuppositions, or assumptions, are also harmful because they cause you to operate on a lack of true knowledge. You may assume that someone hates you because he looked at you angrily one day. You don't realize that he was thinking about his bad day and didn't mean to look at you that way. Always get the full facts before you make a decision. Don't assume that you know how other people think or feel about you, and don't assume that you know all about a situation. Get the full facts before you start beating yourself up or making reckless decisions.

Also, avoid blaming [22]. Some people tend to blame themselves for everything that goes wrong, not realizing that many circumstances are out of their control. For instance, you might blame yourself from someone's death and hate yourself, when you could not have prevented the death no matter what. You must realize that the world does not rest on your shoulders alone.

Others blame other people or life events for everything that goes wrong and don't accept control over their own lives. If you make a traffic mistake and get into a wreck, you blame the other driver for not braking in time. You harbor anger and resentment against everyone and you think that life isn't fair. You don't take control of your actions and apologize when you should. This fills your mind with hatred for the world around you.

You must strike a fine balance when it comes to assigning responsibility to yourself or others. Realize that you can and should take responsibility for your own actions. But sometimes things happen outside of your control. Really ask yourself if something was your fault or someone else's before casting unfair blame on the wrong party. In many cases, all parties were at fault, so there is no use blaming anyone. Instead of trying to find who is at fault or beating yourself up, think about solutions that can make the situation better.

Black and white thinking can drive negativity and bad self-talk, too [22]. This is a cognitive distortion where you feel that things are either all sunshine and rainbows, or all dark and evil. You ignore the gray area that exists in every part of life. For instance, if someone does something bad to you, you think he or she is an evil person. In reality, people are always a mixture of good and bad.

By accepting the fact that things are not black and white, you can stop dwelling on negative emotions like hatred and anger. Let go of the idea that something is all bad and try to find good in it to lessen your reaction to it. You can also stave off reckless optimism that leads to heartbreak and disappointment by accepting that nothing and no one is perfect. There will be something bad or less than ideal about everything and everyone in life. As long as you can focus on the good, you can achieve more positivity and happiness in your attitude.

In some cases, the bad always outweighs the good. If you are dating someone and you can't think of too many good things about him or her, that is a sign that the relationship is not right for you. Instead of blaming yourself or demonizing the other person, simply accept that it is time to move on. Find a healthier situation. Use gray area thinking to recognize when things no longer serve you and you need to move on in life. Don't let bad things fill you with rancor; simply accept that they are bad and that better is waiting for you somewhere else.

Objective Criticism

Pointing out the bad in yourself is not always a bad thing. In fact, it can be quite helpful in driving positive self-growth and change. Objective criticism is the ability to see problems in yourself and address them. It is different from negative self-talk because it is actually helpful. It leads you to find solutions to your behavior and flaws to lead a better life, as opposed to just beating yourself up like with negative self-talk.

An example of objective criticism is the thinking that led you to read this book. You realized that you have a problem with negative self-talk. You recognized that your thinking was causing disturbances in your life and preventing you from being fulfilled. So, you decided to do something about it.

Another example might be when you get into a fight with your spouse. Afterward, you feel awful and you want to say sorry. You see that you did something wrong and you sought to make it right.

Or let's say you are an author. You have sent your book out to a million publishers and received nothing but rejections. As a result, you decide to improve your book. You don't sit there feeling sorry for yourself and thinking that you should give up writing. Instead, you recognized that you have potential but you are missing the mark, so you do something to achieve your goal of publication.

Objective criticism starts with realizing that you are not perfect; no one is. You accept that about yourself and don't let it hurt you. You also forgive yourself and believe in your ability to improve. You know that you have the capability within yourself to become better.

The next part involves identifying a problem or flaw in yourself. Some healthy introspection should reveal a few things that you could fix about yourself. After all, no one is perfect. Even people with high self-esteem are capable of seeing issues within themselves. The crucial difference here between negative self-talk and objective criticism is that you are able to focus on finding a solution, instead of beating yourself up and calling yourself names.

From there, you generate a plan on how you will address this problem and make it better. You set the plan into motion to achieve better results in life. You actively work on it, encouraging yourself and believing in yourself every day.

You may use object criticism on yourself. Or you may receive it from someone else. When you hear someone say something negative about you, you don't get offended, Instead, you choose to use their suggestions as motivation to change. Basically, objective criticism is the same as constructive criticism, except you use it on yourself. You gently point out flaws and suggest improvements.

Objective criticism is useless if you don't use it as a foundation for betterment. Sitting there thinking about how you messed up does not do a single thing. But realizing that you goofed and then taking action to correct that goof is useful. Objective criticism is a powerful tool that can drive positive change within your life.

However, you may also use to accept yourself completely as you are. You may find a few things that you don't necessarily like about yourself. But they have served you thus far. You don't really want to change them. In that case, use object criticism to point out the silver lining to your flaws and embrace them as parts of you. Come to terms with the fact that you are not perfect.

Many people tend to be perfectionists. This only creates the ideal environment for negative self-talk to brew, like bacteria in lukewarm meat. As you set unrealistic high standards for yourself, you are always disappointed. This makes you start to hate yourself because you never live up to your expectations. With objective criticism, you can realize this about yourself and decide to set your standards lower. If you are never good enough, maybe it is time to stop expecting so much of yourself. Accept that you are only human.

However, it is healthy to think, "I am capable of doing the best." That serves as a source of motivation to always do better. By believing in yourself, you eliminate the negative thoughts that lie under perfectionism and instead generate positive thoughts that lie under success.

Objective criticism can also drive good work. Analyze the work you have performed. See where there is room for improvement. Use feedback from others and your own inner critic to make the work as good as it can possibly be. Don't just beat yourself up for not doing something exquisite the first try. Many people with high self-esteem excel in business because they are able to say, "This isn't quite good enough." But they don't just give up and think, "I can never do this." They keep working at it, believing that they can do better. Objective criticism is founded in a sense of confidence, not a sense of inadequacy.

No one enjoys hearing or thinking that he or she is not good enough. But if you speak to yourself nicely and focus on solutions rather than problems, you tend to handle it more gracefully and feel less pain. Just as you would use tact in pointing out something negative to a friend, use tact with yourself. There is no need to critique yourself sharply and harshly. Using gentle language, tell yourself how you can do better and formulate a plan.

You can even use a visualization to picture how you could become the ideal version of yourself or produce better work. Compare reality to your dream. See how they don't match up and then make them match up. Use your inner critic to fuel your motivation to thrive in life.

The Self-Talk Checklist

A checklist can make it easy to redirect your thoughts because you don't have to scramble to remember everything you must do in the construction of positive self-talk. Go down this checklist and see what you did in your positive self-talk. Try to incorporate the elements of the checklist in future positive self-talk.

✓ Is your self-talk stated in the present tense? Talking about the future or the past won't do you any good. The only moment your brain can control is now. Therefore, your self-talk should be based in the present. Think things like, "I am good enough" as opposed to "I will be good enough."

✓ Is it specific?
Your self-talk needs to be specific. Tell yourself exactly what you're good at or what you did well. You will believe it more if it is specific.

✓ Does it get the job done without creating any unwanted side effects?
Self-talk that unintentionally makes you feel bad is still negative self-talk. You might tell yourself something like "I tried my best" which makes you think that you didn't actually do your best, for example.

✓ Is it easy to use?

Self-talk that is not clear or simple will not work. Your brain will have too much trouble processing it, so it won't internalize the meaning behind it and actually believe it. Simple phrases and thoughts are ideal.

✓ Is it practical?

Wildly unrealistic self-talk will only set you up for failure. Focus on things that are tangible and real. For example, telling yourself that you are the best may not be believable, but telling yourself that you are good enough is.

✓ Is it personal?

Your self-talk needs to be about you and things that are profound to you. You need to focus on issues of deep personal significance to yourself. Telling yourself that you are good enough when that is not your real insecurity won't do any good. Find what does cause great insecurity within you and build your self-talk around increasing your confidence in that area.

✓ Is it honest?

Don't lie to yourself. Your self-talk needs to be honest. While it must be positive, it is OK to use objective criticism, as covered in the last section of this chapter.

✓ Does your self-talk ask enough of you?

Self-talk is not helpful if it doesn't push you to succeed. Challenge yourself and really believe that you can rise to the challenge.

✓ Does your self-talk make you feel good?

Your goal with positive self-talk is to encourage yourself to go far. You want to feel lifted up, encouraged, and excited after giving yourself a pep talk. Self-talk that doesn't make you feel good doesn't belong in your mind. Use thought stopping to cease it and find something more positive to center your thoughts around.

✓ Does your self-talk encourage you to go for

better?

You can't love yourself if you don't push yourself to be the best version that you can be. Your self-talk can ask a lot of you, as long as it's realistic and not punishing. Higher expectations can push you to do better. Don't fall into the trap of expecting yourself to be perfect and then beating yourself up when you fall short of those unrealistic expectations, however.

✓ Does your self-talk encourage you to leave or protect yourself from toxic situations?

Self-talk is not helpful if you are simply convincing yourself that a bad situation is good. Acknowledge your true feelings. If someone or something is hurting you, you must believe that you don't deserve it. Stop rationalizing it and acknowledge your pain and your desire for something better.

✓ Do you actually believe it?

If your self-talk sounds hollow and you don't believe it, ask yourself why. You may need to do some introspective exploring to get to the root of your problems.

✓ Do you have evidence to support it?
Evidence can make self-talk more convincing and impactful. For instance, look at a trophy on the wall that you earned or your college diploma. Remember that you earned that. Seek evidence for why you are worthy or good enough or whatever else you are trying to work on.

✓ Are you focused on finding a solution?
If you are talking yourself through a problem, your true goal should be to find a viable solution. Only then can you feel better about your life, because you fixed an issue for yourself. That grows your confidence. Solution-oriented thinking also really helps you take the emotion out of the equation and focus on logic instead, so you feel less hurt and anxious.

✓ Are you trying to find a silver lining in a bad

situation?

Positive self-talk is not the same as denial. If you are in an unpleasant situation, you must get out of it for your own health and safety. Don't let self-talk convince you to ignore red flags and unhappiness.

✓ Are you casting blame on yourself or another person?

As you read before, there is no room for blame. It only causes hard feelings and often it is misplaced. Instead, focus on finding solutions. Don't point fingers at other people and hate them, and don't beat yourself up.

✓ Are you letting go of unwanted feelings?

When you feel negative, that can breed negative self-talk. The best way to stop negative self-talk is to let go of the negative feelings and invite warm, happy feelings. Meditation or visualization or priming can help you achieve this.

✓ Are you stopping negative thoughts and

chasing them with positive ones?

For every negative thought, there is an equally positive one. Identify the negatives ones and chase them with positive ones to make positive thinking a habit. You are reprogramming your brain this way. Identify some common negative thoughts you have and then think of more positive ones that you can use to follow these bad thoughts. Get into the habit of thinking these positives thoughts whenever the negative ones occur.

✓ Are you believing what someone else has said about you?

What people say about you is not true. They don't know you like you know you. While people can offer some valid clues about how you should change, mostly they are taking their own frustrations or insecurities out on you. Don't let negative words get to you and don't let manipulators charm you. Form your own idea of who you are and don't let others influence it, positively or negatively. A sense of independence and separateness from others is essential to staying true to yourself.

✓ Is your self-talk actionable?
Backing your self-talk up with action makes it more effective in changing your life. You will learn more about this, but make sure to have actionable plans when you talk to yourself. Tell yourself how you might address something, or plan a way to treat yourself and make yourself feel better.

✓ Are you motivating yourself?
Before a big show, event, or presentation, it is key to motivate yourself with a little pep talk and some upbeat music. You can also try to use this when you feel anxious about a life event, such as taking a job offer or getting married. Ease anxiety by instead motivating yourself to take action and do something great. Always build yourself up with self-talk when you feel nervous to increase confidence and success, the way Olympic athletes and professional dart players do.

✓ Are you acknowledging your real feelings?

Your real feelings are important clues as to how your life is going. They can alert you to danger, toxic situations, or situations that just aren't the right fit for you at this time. Don't ignore them or soothe them away. Acknowledge them and let yourself feel them. Then tell yourself it's OK to feel that way and find a way to feel better.

✓ Are you speaking to yourself like a friend?

Bad words, insults, and harsh reprimands are not how you should talk to yourself. Stop those thoughts immediately. You must be kind to yourself. Speak to yourself like an old friend that you truly cherish.

Chapter 4: Take Action Now

Positive thinking can bring about some great changes in your life. But it is not going to do a whole lot of good if you don't back positive self-talk and positive thinking with real actions. You can think all day, but only actions will actually trigger positive change in your life.

Positive thinking and positive self-talk can lift the haze of depression that keeps you from taking action. It can also serve as a fantastic source of motivation. It is an excellent place to start in changing your life, which is why it is so crucial to practice.

But now, you need to take it a step further by taking action. Otherwise, your life will not change. You can sit in your armchair and think happy thoughts but that won't make a bit of difference. If you get up and do something to make you happy, however, you will see results. Don't believe that good things come to those who wait. Good things come to those who work for it.

Work for a better life by doing some of the following things.

Make Amends

One major source of the internal conflict that leads to negative self-talk is feeling guilty for some of your less-than-savory actions. All of us have made mistakes, so this does not mean that you are a terrible person. However, the way you handle your mistakes defines how you view yourself and how you feel about your past.

Eliminate regrets and the negative self-talk they generate by making amends for the wrongs you have committed. Say sorry to someone you hurt. Reach out to that old friend that you miss and say "I miss you."

Another thing to do is to ask people for apologies. This may sound crazy because most people who don't love themselves never think to do this. But you can heal a lot of old wounds by telling someone how they hurt you and asking for an apology. You might not hear that apology, but you just got your pent-up anger and hurt off of your chest. Plus, many people don't mean to hurt you and they will be more than happy to make amends to wrongs they didn't mean to commit. Some people may be scared to talk to you after they wronged you, so they appreciate the invitation to be forgiven.

Go After Your Dream Career

A huge act of self-love is finally making that career move that you have been too scared to make. Opening your own business, leaving a corporate job to make art or freelance, leaving your comfortable job of many years for a bigger one, asking your boss for a promotion – these are all scary things. People who don't' love themselves assume that they can't succeed, so they don't take the scary step. They live in fear forever.

However, if you love yourself, you know that you can

do it. You also know that your happiness is not a luxury, but an imperative key to your life. Positive self-talk can help you love yourself enough to take that big step and give yourself something that you really want.

Think about how you want your career to change. Then list the steps you need to make to change it. Put those steps into a plan that you start to work on now. Through deliberate moves, you can make your dreams come true.

When an opportunity comes along, don't hang back in fear. Think, "I deserve this. This is the payout for how hard I've worked." Seize the opportunity and make the best of it.

Fear of the unknown is natural. As your own best friend, however, you will have the confidence to face the unknown. Making a big life change is an act of self-love and you will survive it. Remove the catastrophic sense from the equation and instead think about how great things could be if they worked out. Then take the risk and find out for yourself if this new opportunity is for you or not.

Get Physically Active

Exercise is a simple yet huge act of self-care. There are countless benefits to exercise. For one thing, exercise reduces the stress hormone cortisol, which can make you sleep better and feel better in general [23]. Exercise also stabilizes other hormones, so your mood can improve [23]. On top of weight loss benefits, exercise can increase insulin sensitivity, which can help you absorb nutrients from your food and get nourishment better while banishing tiredness [23]. It can reduce the risk of diseases like Type 2 diabetes and heart disease and even cancer [23]. As your body gets toned, you will have a better self-image and more confidence. You may even make friends at your new workout class or gym.

Most experts recommend at least 150 minutes of exercise per week [23]. How you get this exercise depends on what you like. You will stick to exercise that you enjoy more than something you hate. Any kind of movement will be beneficial in the long run.

Eat Better

Like exercise, eating a good diet is essential to your health and your self-care. You can gain health and lose weight by eating better. Cut out junk food and limit portions. Choose healthy whole foods that you actually like. There is no need to starve yourself or eat health food that you detest, but take care to keep your diet clean. Your sense of well-being and happiness will flourish as you nourish your body the right way. Different people need different diets, so speak to a nutritionist to find the ideal eating plan for your body type and lifestyle.

Start A Fun Hobby

Hobbies are also great for your mental well-being and can relax you after a long day of work or parenting. Doing something that you enjoy is important for your overall health. Find something that you have been wanting to try and try it. If you don't like it, you can stop. Try different hobbies until you find one that you care about.

You should also take an old hobby that you neglected out of busyness. If you miss doing something, make the time to do it. Tell yourself, "I owe this to myself. I can find some time on the weekend to fish again."

Connect With New People

Part of the self-love that comes with positive self-talk involves being more confident and more popular as a result. Your newfound positivity draws people to you. This can make your social life infinitely better.

Take the time to connect with new people. Chat with people you already know but don't connect with much. Call up an old friend. Go out and meet new people with new events or hobbies. As you make more friends, you will feel more likable, which can make you like yourself more. New friends can also open up opportunities for you.

Read A Book Or Watch A Movie You've Been Putting Off

To relax, you should take in a book or movie that you have been wanting to enjoy. Allowing yourself time to enjoy art of some kind is key to unwinding and adding beauty to your life. Just a few minutes to a few hours will renew your appreciation for the world.

In fact, looking at art can have some positive implications for the brain [24]. Art tends to stimulate the release of dopamine in the brain, which makes you feel happier [24]. Art therapy has been used for decades to treat depression, PTSD, anxiety disorder, eating disorders, and other mental health issues for good reason.

Art can range from appreciating a good piece of cinematography to looking at pictures in a gallery. It can involve cozying up with a good book or creating jewelry. Whatever you like that involves art, do it to get a healthy dose of dopamine in your brain.

Travel

Not everyone loves traveling. So if traveling is not for you, there is no need to do it. However, most people have some wanderlust in their hearts. They don't travel out of fear, or because they are too busy, or because they don't have enough money.

Nevertheless, if you start to stop fear and instead build courage with positive self-talk, you can make anything possible. You can find a way to set aside time and raise money for that dream trip. Traveling is a great reward to yourself, to pay yourself back for your hard work and let yourself see the world. It will expose you to new situations and allow you to test yourself, proving a lot to yourself in the process.

Unabashedly Seek Help

If the work required in developing positive self-talk unearths some serious issues, such as mental illness or trauma that you have not healed from, then don't feel ashamed about seeking help.

While a stigma surrounds mental health, there is truly nothing wrong with it. It is better to be healthy and treat mental health issues than to act out on them or let them ruin your life and your relationships. Untreated mental illness can lead to substance abuse, self-harm, suicide, and bad relationships, so you can hurt yourself and others. You can do everyone a favor, including yourself, by committing to a treatment program.

A professional counselor or therapist can help you achieve self-love by offering an outside perspective. A psychiatrist can prescribe medication to aid you in recovering from mental illness and gaining the chemical balance essential to positive thinking.

Use Assertive Language

There are several conversation styles that people adopt [25]. Sometimes, one's style may change, depending on the audience. But the single most effective communication style is assertiveness.

With assertiveness, you are not passive. You tell people what you need or what you feel without fear. However, you do it in a tactful way, not an aggressive way. Hence, you manage to assert boundaries, get what you need, make people respect you, and avoid making enemies or hurting people.

An act of self-care is adopting assertive language. You want to speak firmly. State what you need. Don't hem and haw, but be clear. If something is bothering you, don't hold it in, or act emotionally. Just say what is on your mind and suggest a way to make it better.

It is possible to stage conflict without anyone getting hurt. You can tell people how you feel and ask them to treat you better without yelling, screaming, manipulating, or crying. Such is the beauty of assertive language. You want to be clear about what you are saying. You also want to listen to what your conversation partner says and repeat it back to him to ensure that you get the message.

To speak assertively, make direct eye contact at all times. Speak calmly, without raising your voice, but enunciate clearly. Say what you mean in as few as words as possible; don't make flowery speeches.

Say you feel passed over at work. You can be assertive by asking to speak to your boss. Look him in the eye and say, "I appreciate all that you have done for me and I love working here. But I feel passed over for this project. I feel that I have many things to offer this project, and I should be chosen." Then give your boss time to reply.

Or say your partner carelessly makes a comment about your clothes that hurts your feelings. You can look him or her in the eye and say, "That was hurtful and I don't appreciate it." You don't need to yell, sulk, or cry. Just make your feelings apparent. Give your partner time to apologize and fix what he or she said.

If someone keeps bothering you, you can say, "I really don't like when you do that. Could you please stop?" There is nothing aggressive with that message. It simply gets the message across in an assertive way.

Never level accusations, such as "You keep doing that!"

This puts a person on the defensive. Instead, say, "I don't like when you do that." "I messages" are important in assertive language because it makes what you're saying about you, not about the other person. That removes defensiveness and the need for conflict.

People generally respond well to assertiveness. They like to be given clear directions. Most people will obey what you say if you say it politely but assertively.

Set Boundaries With People

A huge source of unhappiness for most people is a lack of boundaries. Using the assertive language that you learned about earlier, you can draw clear boundaries to keep people from infringing on your values or your personal space. That way, you become happier.

Often, people don't do this because they are afraid of making others not like them. Now that you are your own best friend, you don't need other people to like you to feel validated as a good person. In fact, as you set boundaries in relationships, many people will start to like you more because they can respect you and they know how to act around you.

Your boundaries may be very different from someone else's. It is important to be honest with yourself and get to know the rules you want to set. What bothers you? What is OK and what is not? When people violate these boundaries, firmly but politely speak up and ask the person not to do it again.

End Some Toxic Relationships

It is time to make a list of the people in your life who hurt you. Figure out why each person hurts you. Maybe the problem is you; you take what this person says too personally or you don't communicate well, or you harbor some jealousy because you are engaged in evaluating yourself against this person. But some people are just downright toxic and hurtful, and it is not your fault.

It is crucial to cut these people out of your life. The people who tear you down or make you feel bad when you spend time with them are not good for your health. You don't owe them anything. Do yourself a favor and remove contact with them.

Sometimes, it is not possible to just cut a toxic person from your life. Perhaps you have a co-worker, an in-law, or some other such person that is in your daily life and you cannot create distance. In this case, simply minimize contact and avoid him or her for the most part. When this person hurts you, use visualization to neutralize your feelings and make them less severe and personal. Use a mantra or affirmation to reassure yourself after dealing with this person.

Practice Saying No

Too many people neglect the word "no" in their

vocabulary. You want to please other people to gain validation for yourself. Consequently, you overextend yourself, letting people walk all over you and taking on more tasks than you fit on your plate at the moment. You end up exhausted and regretful at the sharp lack of time you leave for yourself. You feel that no one is truly grateful for all that you do.

Assure yourself that you don't need to make other people like you by doing them favors. Favors only invite people to use you. Instead, you can make people like you by being yourself and letting your good qualities shine through.

Practice looking at your schedule and determining if you really have time to help someone or take on more at work. If a new favor or project cuts into your self-care time, such as your yoga class, put yourself first and say no. Go to yoga. Don't commit to someone else's problems.

You should also say no to things or people that hurt you. If you have a toxic family member who asks to stay, you might feel obligated to say yes, even though you know the stay won't be pleasant. Now, try saying no. Conserve your time and space for yourself and avoid the people who bring you down. If you feel obligated to go to a party but you don't really want to go, then say no. You don't have to please others by showing up to events that you hate.

Practice Saying Yes

While no is a very important word in anyone's vocabulary, so is yes. Too many say no when they want to say yes. They let fear and uncertainty prevent them from agreeing to a situation, person, or opportunity that could potentially change their lives for the better.

Using self-talk, you can gain more confidence and ease social anxiety. This, in turn, can help you find the courage to say yes to that masquerade ball, that new hobby, or that hot date. If you feel a spark in your heart that urges you to say yes, then say yes! Don't let the negative self-doubt make you say no instead.

Conclusion

You are sick of calling yourself names and believing the worst about yourself. Something told you to pick up this book, and now you have all of the tools necessary to reprogram your brain and end the nasty self-talk.

You now know how terrible self-talk is for you. Therefore, you understand it is imperative to switch to positive self-talk. Positive self-talk can make you happier and can enhance your performance in all areas of life. Using it will certainly elevate you to a better lifestyle.

However, just understanding the benefits of positive self-talk won't make it a viable habit. You must use repetition to make it a part of your daily life and enjoy its many benefits. Repeat it every day for 66 days to cement it as a new habit.

Right now, negative self-talk is your habit. It may have

come from an abusive or invalidating childhood, or a traumatic event, or a loss. Whatever the cause, you are not benefiting from it anymore. You can erase the habit of negative thinking and start to enjoy life. Your physical and mental health will improve as a result.

You can reprogram your brain at any age because of neuroplasticity. With mantras, thought stopping, positive affirmations, mental decluttering, and avoiding cognitive distortions, you can reprogram your brain to be more positive. Soon, your instinct won't be to lash out at yourself. You will instead welcome very positive, solution-based approaches to life situations and calm acceptance of painful memories.

You can do most of this work on your own, without paying for an expensive therapist. CBT, visualization, and mental reprogramming are all techniques you can use on your own. However, don't be afraid to reach out for help if you need it. This book is not intended as a replacement for mental health or physical health treatment. To achieve the best results, stick with your current doctors' prescribed interventions and compound them with positive self-talk. You can even find a therapist or counselor who will help you achieve the mental reprogramming necessary for positive self-talk to become a part of your life.

Positive thinking is useless without action behind it. As you begin to talk to yourself as you would a best friend, you will find the motivation to treat yourself with love. This will spill over into your life. You will want to remove toxic situations and friendships from your life, forgive yourself and others, take advantage of great opportunities, and engage in healthy habits that make you happy. You will be able to heal old wounds and make amends. Through a series of actions, you can let positive self-talk make an actual difference in your life.

Be mindful that positivity does not equal happy all of the time. You can criticize yourself and feel pain still.

You just have a healthier way to handle it now.

With positive self-talk, you can open many doors that have been closed for all of your life. Say hello to a bright and wonderful future. It starts today by implementing the techniques covered in these pages!

Resources

[1] Markham, Laura. Peaceful Parent, Happy Kids: How to Stop Yelling and Start Connecting. 2012. TarcherPerigee. ISBN-13: 978-0399160288.

[2] Burnett, Paul. Children's Self-Talk and Significant Others' Positive and Negative Statements. Educational Psychology. 1996. Vol 6, Issue 1. https://doi.org/10.1080/0144341960160105

[3] Kross, Ethan, et al. Self-Talk as a Regulatory Mechanism: How You Do It Matters. Journal of Personality and Social Psychology. American Psychological Association. 2014. Vol. 106, No. 2, 304–324. DOI:10.1037/a0035173

[4]. Yaratan, Huseyin. Self-esteem, self-concept, self-talk and significant others' statements in fifth grade students: Differences according to gender and school type. Procedia - Social and Behavioral Sciences.

2010. Volume 2, Issue 2, pp. 3506-3518
https://doi.org/10.1016/j.sbspro.2010.03.543

[5] Making a Bad Situation Worse: How Negative Self-Talk Worsens Child Anxiety. *Child Anxiety Institute.* http://childrenwithanxiety.com/making-a-bad-situation-worse-how-negative-self-talk-worsens-child-anxiety.html.

[6] Young, Jeffrey & Klosko, Janet. *Reinventing Your Life.* 1994. ASIN: B0776JJ6L8.

[7] Goodhart, D. *Some psychological effects associated with positive and negative thinking about stressful event outcomes: was Pollyanna right?*
Journal of Personal Social Psychology. Vol 48, Issue 1, pp. 216-232. DOI: https://www.ncbi.nlm.nih.gov/pubmed/3981389.

[8] Allan, Scott. *Rejection Reset.* 2017. ASIN: B075JMRTL2.

[9] Zinsser, N., Bunker, L.K, & Williams, J.M. Cognitive techniques for improving performance and building confidence. In J.M. Williams (Ed.), Applied Sport Psychology: Personal growth to peak performance (5th Ed.). McGraw-Hill College, 2006.

[10] Mann, Michael, et al. Self-Esteem in a Broad-Spectrum Approach for Mental Health Promotion. Health Education Research. 2004. Vol 19, No 4, pp. 357-372.

[11] Collingwood, Jane. The Relationships Between Mental and Physical Health. 2018. PsychCentral. https://psychcentral.com/lib/the-relationship-between-mental-and-physical-health/

[12] Raalte, JV. Et al. Cork! The Effects of Positive and

Negative Self-Talk on Dart Throwing Performance. Journal of Sport Behavior. 1995. Vol 18, Issue 1.

[13] Chapman University. New Research on Attractiveness and Mating. ScienceDaily. https://www.sciencedaily.com/releases/2015/09/1 50916162912.htm.

[14] Gardner, Benjamin, et al. Making Health Habitual. British Journal of General Practice. 2012. Vol 62, No 605, pp. 664-666.

[15] Jones, MD, et al. A naturalistic study of fat talk and its behavioral and affective consequences. Body Image. 2014. Vol 11, No 4, pp. 337-345. doi: 10.1016/j.bodyim.2014.05.007.

[16] Miller, Kevin, et al. Habits without Values. Cold Spring Harbor Laboratory. 2018. doi: https://doi.org/10.1101/067603.

[17] Demartini, John. The Demartini Method. https://drdemartini.com/about/demartini-method/

[18] Robbins, Tony. How Should I Start Each Day? What's   Priming? https://www.tonyrobbins.com/ask-tony/priming/

[19] Bandler, Richard. The Ultimate Guide to NLP: How to Build a Successful Life. 2013. HarperCollins. ISBN-13: 978-0007497416

[20] Schacter, Daniel L., et al. The Future of Memory: Remembering, Imagining, and the Brain. 2013. Neuron.   Vol   76,   No   4. doi: 10.1016/j.neuron.2012.11.001

[21] Stop Negative Thoughts. *Michigan Medicine.* 2019.   https://www.uofmhealth.org/health-library/uf9938.

[22] Wolf, Alex. *Cognitive Behavioral Therapy: An Effective Practical Guide for Rewiring Your Brain and Regaining Control over Anxiety, Phobias, and Depression.* ISBN13: 9781726691222.

[23] *Benefits of Exercise.* MedlinePlus. https://medlineplus.gov/benefitsofexercise.html

[24] Regev, Dafna, et al. *Effectiveness of Art Therapy in Adults in 2018 – What Progress Has Been Made?* Frontier Psychology. 2018. Vol 9, p. 1531. DOI: 10.3389/fpsyg.2018.01531

[25] Newton, Claire. *The Five Conversation Skills.* Web. N.d. http://www.clairenewton.co.za/my-articles/the-five-communication-styles.html.

Disclaimer

The information contained in this book and its components, is meant to serve as a comprehensive collection of strategies that the author of this book has done research about. Summaries, strategies, tips and tricks are only recommendations by the author, and reading this book will not guarantee that one's results will exactly mirror the author's results.

The author of this book has made all reasonable efforts to provide current and accurate information for the readers of this book. The author and its associates will not be held liable for any unintentional errors or omissions that may be found.

The material in the book may include information by third parties. Third party materials comprise of opinions expressed by their owners. As such, the author of this book does not assume responsibility or liability for any third party material or opinions.

The publication of third party material does not constitute the author's guarantee of any information, products, services, or opinions contained within third party material. Use of third party material does not guarantee that your results will mirror our results. Publication of such third party material is simply a recommendation and expression of the author's own opinion of that material.

Whether because of the progression of the Internet, or the unforeseen changes in company policy and editorial submission guidelines, what is stated as fact at the time of this writing may become outdated or inapplicable later.

written expressed and signed permission from the author.

Lightning Source UK Ltd.
Milton Keynes UK
UKHW040645110320
360160UK00001B/218